PORTABLE PLANET

Also by Eric Paul Shaffer

RattleSnake Rider   (LongHand Press)

kindling: Poems from Two Poets   (LongHand Press; co-author, James Taylor III)

How I Read Gertrude Stein by Lew Welch   (Grey Fox; editor)

Instant Mythology   (Backer Editions)

PORTABLE PLANET

POEMS

ERIC PAUL SHAFFER

*For Luis + Cindy Urrea —
Welcome to the planet!
Enjoy your visit!
Best,
your pal
Eric*

Leaping Dog Press

CHANTILLY, VIRGINIA : 2000

ISBN 1-58775-000-7 (paper)
ISBN 1-58775-001-5 (electronic)
Library of Congress Catalog Number: 00-108699

This book has been printed on recycled, acid-free paper, by McNaughton & Gunn, Saline, MI, and has been published in an edition of 1,000 copies, of which the first 100 are signed and numbered by the author.

This is number _____ of 100.

Leaping Dog Press
PO Box 222605
Chantilly, VA 20153-2605
www.leapingdogpress.com

Acknowledgments

I gratefully acknowledge the editors of the following fine publications for previously printing many of the poems in this book: *ACM (Another Chicago Magazine), Bakunin, California State Poetry Quarterly, Chaminade Literary Review, East & West Quarterly, The MacGuffin, Pearl, Pinchpenny, Pleiades, Poetry Motel,* and *Stick.* As for the rest of you, the work's in the mail.

A special thanks to Sara Backer of Backer Editions for publishing *Instant Mythology,* a small chapbook of my work, in 1999. Thanks also to Georgette Perry for including my work in her anthology, *Witnessing Earth: Poems of Nature and the Sacred* (1994), and to James Taylor III for including my work in his forthcoming anthology, *On Fry Bread & Poetry.*

Greetings and gratitude to all, and especially to these eminent humans: Veronica Winegarner, Jordan Jones, Jim Harrison, Bill Porter, Steve Sanfield, Magda Cregg, John Kain, James Taylor III, Cheri Crenshaw, David Robertson, P. D. Murphy, Sean O'Grady, Suzi Winson, and as always, Lew Welch and the *Ancient Order of the Fire Gigglers.*

DIRECTIONS: As a literary supplement, peruse three pages daily. Remove inner seal. Twist off. Squeeze. Heat to boil. Stir vigorously. To preserve quality and freshness, crack volume regularly. Expose to light. Open here.

CAUTION: CONTENTS UNDER PRESSURE.

This volume is designed for all poetry readers and makes ten thousand and one suggested-strength 3-page servings. Your satisfaction with this poetry is guaranteed, and questions or comments about these poems are welcome. When writing, include ISBN on back of volume. Send correspondence to eshaffer@hotmail.com.

Best when purchased immediately. Not for resale.

Contents

PORTABLE PLANET

for Veronica,
my Rock

summer, night, *Pulau Seribu*

Tonight, we discover fire in black
waves burning on sand
in starshine, breaking and becoming
                green, luminous.

The sea glows with life feeding
on flow, thriving in windy surf,
        rising with tides on dark beaches

        the moon makes bright.

The Ecology of a Portable Planet

T his volume is composed of three books. Each was originally intended as a separate work and can stand alone.

Familiar, Far is closest in vision to where I was when *RattleSnake Rider,* my second book of poetry, was published in 1990. That work was grounded in the western United States, particularly the great central valley of California. Though composed in the same spirit, many of these poems were written on Okinawa, after I left America but before I was familiar enough with Japan to write about it. The lines recall days when I could walk the railroad tracks with my dog at dawn, then drive down to Mt. Tamalpais to watch vultures.

The Western Room is a long poem presented as a tour of the grounds of Shuri Castle, less than a mile from our apartment on Okinawa. I began writing it within a month of our arrival, and throughout our eight years on the island, I incorporated my deepening awareness of the place and my place within it. As the heart of a lost kingdom, the castle appealed to me, and I spent many afternoons sitting by the royal pond. For me, the poem is a record of sudden insights and strange shifts in perspective and perception that accompany long residence in a foreign country to which one is also foreign.

The Rush Through Blue is a volume of poems written in Japan and clearly inseparable from the East. Many of the works present both America and Japan as foreign and reveal the ambiguities in the stance of a speaker without a land to stand on. They are gathered here because most feature images, events, people, and ideas from the many nations I visited during the eight years I lived in Japan, and all of them speak of times I would not have otherwise known. I would never have penned these words had I not crossed the Pacific to live on the edge of Asia.

The arrangement of the books and the sequence of poems in this volume should not restrict the freedom of readers. Presenting poems in a book requires an order, no matter how arbitrary, and this one satisfied my sense of design. Start anywhere. Start everywhere. Welcome to the planet.

EPS
July 1, 1999
on the slope of Haleakala, Maui

i: FAMILIAR, FAR: OPEN LETTERS

At Play in the Fields of the Word

At the oak, the sun covers eyes and counts.
Nobody hides.
          The neighborhood is silent.
A weekday, and the world is away.
              I'm at home at work, awake,
at the kitchen table, reflecting on the toaster.

These are days without fame.
       None come to the door
              but grim vendors
of an angry God and trademark plasticware.

I sit all day, lone, new pen still,
        a pole to ring
     with words tossed, off-hand, glib,
        on decks of empty white reams,
and only myself to fill them.

In the yard are toys
scattered by children fluent in games of genius
        and swift gestures of creation
halted by a father's sharp whistle through the dusk.
      Balls, rings, and hoops lay lost.

Alone, with nothing but a window
                  and a world to gaze on,
I am the dictionary of my own destiny.
          Today, I define *freedom* this way:
        with nothing done, the future is full.

Outside the kitchen door,
             under limitless blue
       unlined by clouds, all is clear.
The planet is my house. I'm at home
       in my own backyard.

The swings hang slack. The slide
         mirrors morning. The grass
gleams wild, grown thick through the fence.

         Let us play
before the children and the critics come.

Welcome to the Planet

a greeting to newborn humans

This day, we welcome you.
We teach our ways to greet you.

We are one kind among many the world encircles.
Touch all gently.

Our people are near us always.
Find yourself among the best.

Cities display our inventions and designs.
Watch, wonder, and wander away.

Highways are dark and long, concrete and crowded.
Make your own way.

Birds and beasts bring news of the planet.
Good news for your ears only.

The sea foretells the past and future.
Live now.

Soil is the source of the great and the humble.
See the small creatures close.

Mountains reveal nothing lasts.
Make peace with this.

Rivers flow in the direction of days.
Mark the many courses well.

Woods are where the world breathes.
Breathe deeply.

We greet you as your way begins.

Welcome to the planet.
Welcome home.

Clawed Tracks: Michigan, 1971

No wolf prowls this forest.
No owl questions my presence
in stillness frozen beneath drifts of icy white.
The sound of my passage does not disturb pine boughs
laden with patient showers of snow:
I am no intruder here
in these hallowed places men fear for their silence
and even the wind refuses to speak.

I roam between trunks that promise summer
and hang the green threat of youth
iced white by January stark above my head.
My trail is a series of clawed tracks
that will grow in the spring thaw
and hunters will be unable to explain.

A Blessing for *The California Kid*

after J.K. writes that The California Kid, the twenty-two-year-old
motorboat we restored, is sold to a nice, old fishing couple,
and asks me to pen the final prayer

Bless your bow for parting the waters before us and your wake
for revealing the point of passage
on our pathless way along the shore,

bless your foredeck, for the white paint bore the symbol
of good company in a dark time,

bless your not-so-secret compartment beneath the foredeck,
for the hold held the beer well
and kept the good brew cold,

bless your windshield, for the curved plastic scattered the spray
of rough waters and the cold winds of fortune and speed,

bless your wheel for teaching us to choose our own direction
with our lives in our hands,

bless your braces and beams, for they gave us comfort

and strength in our times of need,

bless your lights, bow and stern, for burning bright,

marking our position and direction
in the darkness on the waters,

bless your anchor for simple utility and standing firm

in the rare need on the gentle rivers we rode,

bless your lines for taking good knots, holding you fast to the dock

for our certain return,

bless your short, ragged rope for starting the engine on the first

or the second pull,

bless your ancient engine for driving us surely through the current

and open waves,

bless your red tank for storing fuel enough to discover new places

and always return,

bless your propeller for whirling three broad wings underwater,

driving us through the elements,

bless your pistons for proving

the true two-stroke rhythm powering the universe,

bless your points and plugs for teaching timing means running smoothly

and a slow pace makes the best time
with nowhere to go,

and bless the waters where you shone day and night,
    stony bottoms we scraped going a little too far,
   pebbled banks where the dog shook the river from his fur,
     nights we drank down dark drifting with beer and stars,
    and the sacred day the salmon swam beneath the bow:

  we wish you fine fortune, *California Kid*, long may you run.

Cougar and Rocks,
Yosemite National Park

a photograph for David Robertson

Gary Snyder says in his life he's seen three —
treeing one with a flashlight
and Masa walking home to Kitkitdizze in the dark.

But driving this daylight I'm unwilling to see what I know
is before me,
considering how desperately we all want to see Cougar.

Coyote feasting on Doritos
at the crossroads was such a surprise
my eyes got dull to the wild in the park.

But that's not Coyote over there by those rocks.
(wrong gait, no attention for cars)
Bobcat? Lynx?
(Lynx, so *impossible*! Bobcat, too small!)

big cat rolling shoulder, flip-flat foot stride,
tail tipped black

(When my friends tell this story, I say,
"It was a *huge* bobcat — and what a long *tail!*")

but now I am possessed
beating the window with my fist till the car stops
and I jump out running
across the field to see better.

(color right, size right, location right —
it *must* be!
but can't see enough —
damn, left binoculars and camera on the front seat)

Cougar reaches the rocks
sauntering in while I'm still
running a hundred feet behind
then looks over a shoulder, down a tawny back,
lashes that tail once,
and disappears.

I stop — smart enough at least not to follow into rocks.

My friends call me back to the road.
A family not far away picnics in the grass
watching *me* with wary eyes.

I'm alone now in a meadow with mountain, sky, trees, and sun —
who will watch me go
when I turn away?

Far from the House, I Climb

Alone in the snow,
among pines, far from the house,
I climb.

Up a thin bole, snapping limbs, flaking
trunks, higher than the hilltop
our old house settles in.

I see winter blue through brown
cones and thick green needles,
and struggle up quick, then stuck.

What is solid, sways.
I'm a white monkey wondering in air.
How did I climb into cloudless blue?

Look around. The house, the hill.
The tree trembles, tilts,
shaking snow onto snow.

Gazing down the bole
at branches and bark
darkening drifts, I trace

my blank-soled footprints
backward through snow
I crossed from high, heated,

knotted, wooden rooms, leaving.
From one tree among lines of pines
in Michigan woods,

a forest is a history, a family
treed by rising too far —
a trunk too thin,

branches too thick to mount further.
I almost hear the hounds. The house is lost
in branches, and I freeze to the tree.

I can ascend no higher.
Deer browse the limbs below.
I cling to the trunk

as did ancestors of ancient descent,
lithe little climbers with wide eyes and brains
too big to bear,

waiting while the tree, the world, grows
large enough, or dark enough,
to deliver me.

A Note on the Diligence of Janitors

During the Earth Day Festival someone stuck a sticker —
a silver-dollar-sized picture of the Earth
as the world appears from space —
on top of the toilet tank.

For the longest time, it was the first thing you saw
when you answered nature's call.

There it was — green, blue, brown, and silly on stark white —
one simple glimpse of the gleaming world
before turning your back
to squat down to business.

Today, I saw the world again after ages.

The janitor scrubbed the surface of that flat planet raw.
Now, a second face shows below —
clouds and continents lose their shape,
land glows red and seas boil brown.

From this grimy, blank tank of hissing water, persistent
tinkles, gurgles and subterranean bubbles,
the janitor's job is to make everything
go smoothly
down the drain.

Indian Petroglyph State Park,
Albuquerque, New Mexico

About the time my ancestors were hauling marble around
for some cathedral in Europe
or making paintbrushes for Michelangelo,
somebody who knew this place
squatted before this black volcanic rock
chipping this design onto this face.

Meaning maybe a star shone brightly overhead here
or marking a significant event at this intersection
of the ten directions — a solstice, a vision, a falling star,
an uncommon bird.

A patient hand made these images without a plan —
thoughtfully unaware that Christians crossing the sea
would build a fence around this *malpais*
and make this ground a park.

Today, I saw my first Loggerhead Shrike —
black mask, thick dark beak, silver head, black wings
with a shock of white in the unfurling —
perched on a wire fence
next to a lizard impaled on a barb,
just like the book says.

On The Often Unremarked
Advantages of Baldness

What grows up must go bald.
Yet from this hairless height,
>   gleaming vistas of the future appear
when you boldly glow where no skin has shown before.

See what I mean? The glory of the sun
>   sets the shedding head ablaze.
The horizons of one's sense of humor
>   broaden as swiftly as hairlines recede,
for the bald head is the bare butt
>   of every joke.

Look around.
Everyone sees the naked truth sparkling on the scalp.
>   There's no point in splitting hairs,
and the bald facts have their benefits:

One may amass
>   without criticism
>   a spectacular collection of goofy hats.

No one ever forgets the color of your eyes.

The bald man knows rain falls
        with the shock of the first drop.

One may chant with brats in the schoolyard:

   "No more shampoo, no more comb,
      no more hair upon my dome.
   No more haircuts, no more styles,
      no more nasty barber smiles."

A gleam from the bean grants license to revise
the accidental anthems of youth — apologies to CSNY.
      Sing along:

   "Almost bought some hair,
      it happened just the other day.
   Gettin' kinda bald, 's gonna buy myself a toupée.
      But I didn't, and I wonder why.
   I feel like letting my sun-spot shine.
   I feel I should show it to someone."

Scholars even teach
Wisdom herself reigns within the tonsure
      Age clips around the crown.
And spiritually, the time-shorn shine head and shoulders
   above the rest. The empty pate
is the glossy sign of the pure at heart.

Bald, you may be humbled by the true dimensions
      of the skull,
but a certain resemblance to the cosmic egg
   leads many to believe men of radiant cranium
more enlightened than they really are.

The sheer error in such assumptions is plain enough,
　　　　　but with little thought,
the skullful may turn this to advantage
　　　　by keeping the head bowed
　　　　and the mouth shut.

Silly youth may hallow
　　　　the hollow halo on your head,
may salute the colors of aged skin brave against the sky
　　　　for a few amusing years,
before Death creeps in with rusty scissors
to clip the naked skull so close
　　　　a headstone fits like a marble hat,
and from your hairless head, at last, grows grass.

Good Odds

In Las Vegas tonight, far from home, half-asleep,
        I wonder about the day I die,
    and a date comes to mind.

Should I never fly that day? Stay home? Not drink?
        Always eat seconds of my favorite meal?
    Never fail to make love the day before?

Now, I'm wide awake in a strange motel room
        with all the lights on,
my life flashing before my eyes on the Great Bright Way.

As long as I live, the day I die doesn't matter,
        but do I say, "Hit me,"
    and simply get on with my life?

I stare at check-out time scrawled in black
        behind a rented door in Nevada.
The air-conditioner is broken, and I'm choosing sides:
    "DO NOT DISTURB" or "MAKE UP THIS ROOM EARLY."

If I play my cards right, I'll stand pat
        for the eternal Whatever,
a prodigy of preparation for the inevitable.

If I'm wrong, there are 364 other chances every year,
                    and one more on leap year,
        to hold the hand I'm dealt before I fold.

Every day is wild. I'll live each as my last.
        There are good odds one day I'll be right.

Love & Hate Crimes

seven short subjects and change

I.   Why Basic Training is Worse Than Hell

       "In hell, you know you deserve it."

II.   Real Men

       There's a name for tanned, slender men
          who wear pretty red scarves, fancy hats,
             tight jeans,
       and pointy-toe, high-heel, shiny leather boots:
          cowboys.

         Hello, Wyoming!
         Chew *that* cowchip.

III.   Creative Writing

a course poem

The difference
between cheating and creating
is a roll of the tongue
and aspiration.

IV.   Inter-Species Communication

"Everybody tells me to love my brother.

"Well, I can't stand that bastard.
Hell, sometimes, I can't even stand my damn *friends*!

"Let me tell you what I mean.

"Just yesterday some stupid fucking kid
in the Bronx got two polar bears killed
because he climbed *in*to their cage
over a twenty-foot chain-link fence
on a dare."

V.   Synchronicity In My Pants

My favorite poet happened
to find my lover's
on-again-off-again-ex-boyfriend's birthday
a great day for poetry and letters.

Damn.

She's seeing him again now. I just *know* it.

The round Zen monk

swats at winged infinity

buzzing past his shaven pate

on the orange self-portrait

covering new collected poems.

"Isn't that annoying?"

Now, I'll *never* be able to think

of that poetry

without making this connection again.

bzzzzzzzzzzzzzzzzzzzzzzzz.

VI.   Mt. Rushmore Soliloquy

"See, that's that guy on the quarter,

the guy on the penny,

that guy on the god-damn two-dollar bill,

and I don't know who

the guy in glasses is."

VII.   An Achronological Cyclical History of a Man
In a Short List of Ridiculous Phrases,
Or Words to Clear the Tongue Before Reading Poetry

a tune prune for Lew

"baby suck"

bald skull

light bulb

lady bucks

VIII.   The Taylor/Ginsberg Moment

James met Ginsberg.

Ginsberg said, "Y'got a cigarette?"

James, "No, but I got matches."

This is the life.

Instructions for Your First Poem

for Kelia and all

This is your first poem. You can use it for many things.

It may keep you dry in a sudden storm.
                        You can take notes on it.
              Make a list. Fold it and let it fly.

You can see through it. It's a window to this world.

You can learn to read with it. It may teach you
                    colors and numbers and shapes.
You can review the sounds of farm animals with it.

Do not use it wisely or sparingly. Don't be careful with it.
              Bend, fold, and articulate.

You can use a poem over and over and over
                    again.
              It will always be the same.

Mark it in pencil like a familiar door-jamb.
Every year, when you stand next to it,
　　　　you'll see how much you've grown.

The Poet Cancels My Birthday

for S. G.

My friends call to apologize
     for my age,
forgetting cards,
        or for getting cards.
Old girlfriends leave messages
they think of me sometimes
when they make love,
and now they're glad
       they're gone.
The dog has diarrhea,
and the cat's chin won't heal
     from her clawing for fleas.
The left rear tire's flat again,
and I lent the jack to somebody
     who forgot to bring it back.
Last night, I lost my best
       blue sweater.
This morning, there are no maple doughnuts,
the coffee tastes especially bad,

and the paper says the poet's farewell
        tonight is canceled.
But walking the dog early,
        I passed a vacant parking meter
ticking away as furiously as tomorrow will —
fifty-five minutes to go
        and not a car in sight.

Rime for Mr. Frost

a triolet for the end of the world

Some favor fire to end the world.
                    Cold is kinder.
From life to light in flames unfurled,
some favor fire to end the world.
Yet the last will see, in darkness whirled,
Cold holds all one: ageless binder.
Some favor fire to end the world.
             Cold is kinder.

Rage Against the Dying

lest we speak ill of the dead

Let us say that my father died of an excess
of wind
in a wilderness of gray scrub and black branch.
His soul passed in a blast
of bad air from puckered lips,
a single word spoken low —
he never knew the meaning nor the loss.

Let us say my father died of amnesia,
forgetting all but his own pain,
all but his own little wishes.
Crouching on his crooked crag,
he tallied the tiny slights
flesh makes heirs of in the mortal coil
and flex of beating a path through life
toward a destination devoutly to be.

Let us say my father died holding his breath
in the dark

until his brain expired,
his last intelligence pacing back
and forth between the gray walls
of locked cells in his cerebral cortex,
        never to stalk, never to pounce,
a tiger crazed by confinement,
        burning bright.

Let us say my father died of rage
        when his enemies grew up
or died of grief at his constant retreats.
        With their work and their children,
his children let him be.
                His wife died
believing he was all her fault. He cursed her
for leaving him as he left her.

Let us say my father died of bitterness.
What galled the man was what
        we learned from him —
exactly what not to be, just what not
        to do, the perfect words to withhold
when tempers rise like hot rockets
                on Independence Day.

Let us say my father died of curses
he taught, teaching us not to curse
what we don't understand, not to hope
        for the worst, not to forgive
and not forget, not to hit, kick, punch,
whip with belts, boards, cords,
                and not to slap
since stupidity thrives in us all.

Let us say my father died of shame
that those he hurt forgave, forswore,
                    or forgot him.
Alone with his crimes, he cried.
                Forgiven, he wished for more.
Denied, he attacked those who knew him
        too well for him to wound.

Let us say my father died of anger
when his children refused him his crown,
        a crown he dreamed on the road,
driving highways half-asleep,
a gaudy thing gone but not forgotten
in the sudden swerve of the newest,
                nearest missed collision.

Let us say my father died of embarrassment
                    seeing his children saw him
as a clown, a joey, a flirt, a fart, a jester
far more worthy of motley and a coxcomb.
He cursed them all
        and settled for nothing.

Let us say, then, my father died for nothing,
cracked, haggard, thick around the middle,
wheezing for wind, slack of skin and limb —
        broken pipes blown out by the gods
of rage, winded and worn, ripped, tossed, lost
            on a littered field of living
my father always saw as battle.

So, let us say my father died with the wind
still carrying his cries and curses,
unholy shrieks scraping a gray slate of sky,
wandering the blasted heath
                    of his imagination,
shaking a fist of rage reasonlessly
in the face of those close enough
        to curse, to kiss, or to kick.

How I Read Poetry

When I finish reading
the book

I crumple
      the sales slip
   I used
to mark my place

and throw it away.

America, In Your Name ...

I found my name. In the heart of the nation, I stood,
proud, through long years of pledging allegiance.
    The delight of discovery straightened my spine
and set my hand above my heart.

In every classroom we faced the flag,
                I learned the character of my country
                   in the shaky grace
    I pressed into letters of lead.

Grade to grade, I traveled roads of blood
              through bars of blankness
    and lost my way in fields of midnight
        and a regiment of stars.

The blue-bannered constellation beyond me then
                     now falls away.
In this twilight, the land is not the nation,
    and a name is simply shared territory.

At last, I stand in familiar wilderness
built of bones and charts and letters and latitude,
              on ground I cannot claim,
    lost in a place I must name myself.

Three Lost and Ancient Mythical Kingdoms

I. Animal

These breathe. Wind moves
visibly in their chests.

Ribs rise and fall as breeze blows through
blood and bone of the cow,
        the whale, and the wolverine.

Animals are made of air,
walking clouds,
        living breath
shaped by the wind of the world.

First breath flows inward.

II. Vegetable

Green, they grow for light, explosions
        of protoplasm from the ground
            up.

One place is all they know.
They go nowhere. Seeds travel
      in shells, in streams, in hair,
in the pebbled guts of birds.

Water grown strong
      in stem, fiber, and root,
        sun gone green in branch, bud, bloom.

Sap is sweet dark flow to flower.

III.   Mineral

These wait.
Every part of the planet
      is this patient stuff.

In mountains, minerals mock
    the other kingdoms
built on them, built of them.

Layers of the lost, bone turns stone.
      The last leaves, limb and shell,
the faint shape of the past
        hidden, hardened.

Food for the tiniest, home for the rest,
everlasting, elemental
     material.

Plotting for Feathers,
Scheming for Scales

"I don't really like birds. They're practically reptiles."
— Lew Welch as Abner

All winter long,
      RattleSnake knots a plot for feathers,
    dreams coiled round darkness, tail on tongue.
Crow yearns to squirm through the world on his belly,
        aware the crust is the rind of Earth
with sweet juices bubbling down deep.

RattleSnake sees the world on the wing,
      aloft above Mt. Tam's peak,
    and traces the serpentine curve of Earth
through the unseen force of the third element,
viewing what the Moon sees
    in 28 fine faces of shadow and light.

Crow shivers through winter
      asnooze in the sky, hungry,
learning the stomach is a drum the gods beat
    with the bones of those they starve.
Black back bent against gray, Crow groans.
   Taut claws clasp cold wire.

RattleSnake rounds the season's circle,
     seeing sky shift from lead to lapis lazuli.
Rocks shock the falling, but one who walks
          wind beyond the reach of stone
enters a zone only fire tops. His length lifts,
    loops through wind, drifts lazily to zenith.

Power sparks dark dreams in wet, black feathers.
        Asleep,
Crow seeks the Earth's molten core.
Within, warm, sweet, light, seeds of the planet ripen.
    There, everything that moves,
        flies.

The Year of the Dog

to Rufus, in four elements

I.   Earth

My only claim is to share the hallowed ground.

James buried my dead dog on rented premises
                at 13,000 feet —
somebody's abandoned summer-house dream —
      near the bones of his own dead dog,
           too close to the propane tank.

Snow glows on the Continental Divide,
          banners flying from the peaks,
    seen atop that cold stack of stones.

      "Down, boy, back into the planet!
          Lie down."

II. Fire

I never saw Rufus by firelight. Imagine!
      You live good long days with a dog,
    and then, he's gone. Not even a gleam.

Fire, he feared not, but from lightning, he bolted.
    The flashes were bad. Thunder, too much.
         BOOM!

That dog streaked for the bed —
          under the sheets head-first
charming his way to the safest spot he knew.

    Furry tremors at every flaming fork
till I pulled a blanket over his head, and he slept.

III. Water

That dog loved water, though. I always thought
      I would bury him at sea.

Reckless, Rufus, and the waves of the rolling ocean —
   "C'mon now, dog!
    Into the animal soup, boy! Jump!"

But rivers were his first love. He caressed the waters
with his tongue, chest-deep in the American River,
     drinking, drinking till his gut bulged.
        Then, he would waddle out
and mark every ragged riverbank cottonwood.

    Was he only trying to get to the other side?

IV. Wind

Rufus always reminds me of autumn and twilight,
his fur, the color of fallen leaves, dry, stiff,
    a crushed, rusty mosaic of the lines in your hand.

My old neighbor burns heaped leaves in his backyard —
      a tang of smoke in clothes, in nose,
chill on cheek, tear blown from an eye by the wind.

Look! There's Rufus running in early purple dusk.

    Orange tongues leap through low blue smoke.
Fire darts from the heart of a rough, brown mound —

    "Hey, mister, stand back! Out of the way!
      Can't you see my dog
          is flying?"

The Image That Must Remain

for Sheila

She stands in sunlight rippled by shadows of leaves
        beneath an orange tree in southern California.

A lucky day in June. Rain gone, sun come
        on the day of her birth: seven years ago today.

She is the center of a circle of laughter,
        with *piñata* suspended from a branch above.

Her eyes are bound. Her horizon, the bright bandana
        her grandfather sent from El Salvador.

Spun, she loses her place and direction. Released, she whirls,
        swinging at the gaudy paper prize —

a hornéd beast of burden bearing gifts within
        knotted crepe of red, blue, green, and gold.

She laughs, and our laughter inspires her as she seeks
　　　　　the bright bounty above her head

with a wooden stick straight and sturdy for wild swings
　　　　　through the promise of summer.

The hem of her dress blooms in a ring spun from the vigor
　　　　　in her pivots, her leaps, her play.

At last, she breaks the hollow body of the beast and finds herself
　　　　　in a shower of sweets and silver.

In this moment, we celebrate living and glimpse the essential.
　　　　　This is the image that must remain:

The little girl spins till we lose count of the turns,
　　　　　and she loses all sense of herself.

Blinded by the material, she seeks and reaches
　　　　　for the wonder we hope awaits her.

I wish her always the joy of this day.
　　　　　I wish her vision in the days to come.

What the World Says

by Kathryn Capels and Eric Paul Shaffer

I've been listening a long time
        to what the world says —

Humans are fat carp feeding at the bottom
        of oceans of air.
        Bread is the bait they take best.

Straight lines exist only in the human head.
        Waves. Just waves.

The shortest distance between two points
        is math,
        not as the crow flies.

Fire is friend to wood, metal, and earth.
        Water is its mate.

Bears do not rule the planet
                only because they are wise enough
        to sleep through winter.

If there is magic, there is no safety.
                If there is safety, there is no magic.
        These words are tattooed on the soles
           of my feet.
               Watch me walk.

A Perforated Ode to the "E" Stamp

I. The E Stamp on Earth

Hail to thee, E Stamp! All honor to you,
Triple-Horned Letter of Plenty! Long live
the Capital Stamp of First Class Communication!
Grant us favor, O Two-Dimensional Servant of Hermes!

You are my stamp of the world!
Able and willing to bear our words through the nation thus far
and no further —
so domestic, so provincial, so petulant, so USA!

O, E Stamp, your four-square abbreviation is no mystery to me.
Your origins are as plain as the world on your face.

Earth,
(labeled carefully below — there can be no mistake!),
your face is familiar:
Hooray, for the green, white, and blue!

O Earth, your face inked a billion times
in perfect lines on perforated plates
impresses us, tearing planets apart,

licking sticky backsides, and thumbing
ragged squares into bright corners
of an ordered universe of correspondence
where mail arrives on time, there are no strikes,
and nobody ever raises rates
on letters, capital or otherwise.

Earth, shine this way always in our postage:
bright blue buckle on a grand band of fire,
electric orange, yellow, and white light
gleaming in stars and universal blue.

My fellow Americans, try this!

Squint through whirling continents and clouds.
Can you see where you live? I see
the Sacramento flowing through the valley.
The I Street bridge. Fishermen nodding on houseboat decks.
Hey, there's a couple of salmon!

Ready or not, here I come.
Look out below!

II.   The E Stamp of Approval

Consider the enigma of the E stamp
and the planet for which it stands,
one postage understood as one big E and just an E for all:
a capital letter of unknown worth.

O, E Stamp, hear my plea!
Let there be correspondence between us.

Let me fully illustrate the stamp of the world. Let the E stamp me.
Let me symbolize Earth, wandering, chaos and cosmos
wild within a blue-green skin glimmering
with continents and seas, a slick, sticky surface gleaming with life.

Let me be the E in Empyrean, clear cosmic shell
at the edge of the universe.
Let me punch my head through to the music of spheres.
I'll send a postcard: "Wish you were here!"

Let me spin through space, tell the times,
and pen new letters on blue-ruled lines. Let me draw
lines littered with letters slit open and read, running
with blood and breath in a thin script
of famous last words scraped on paper
with the sharp point of a pen.

Let me stomp a roulette on the face of the Earth,
every print of my sole a hole in the world,
piercing ears, hearts, planet, skies, eyes, paper, and breath.

Let me tear along the dotted line —
if it hurts, bear it;
if it tears, rip it; if it rips, lick it raw, stick it
in a corner, and address it to me —
from the hole in your head to the hole in mine.
In the E posted through a flat blue world pressed to paper,
I'll finally see what's become of me.

Let me find myself in the heart of America,
a perforated man seeing stars
from a planet printed with postage marked E,
a grand character gleaming through clouds above
with a message and meaning ambiguous as love.

III.   The E Stamp Acts

O, E Stamp, holy perforated postal square,
thin paper bridge spanning a planet,
I dedicate myself to you. As you serve, so shall I serve
to transport words, to translate sense into every sense.
E stamp, you are my bond,
my proof I've paid the postage due
for the privilege of daily delivery.

And Earth, blue two-bit planet of my birth, my words
are insured to post you on your appointed rounds
with destination writ large
and a litter of poems swelling the belly of the epistle you bear,
me, writing the world, bearing witness.

O, E stamp,
I am your open letter to the world.

ii: THE WESTERN ROOM

"It is even stranger to be the man who weaves
words in a room, in a house."

— Jorge Luis Borges

•

In Japan, all is defined as "Japanese style" or not. *Wafu* is "Japanese-style," and *youfu* is "Western-style." One never mistakes one for the other.

When I first entered the apartment in the government housing complex where I was to live for the next six years, my Japanese colleague walked me proudly from room to tiny room.

"There are two *washitsu* and one *youshitsu*."

He pointed to two rooms floored with *tatami* mats.

"Those are Japanese-style."

Then, he nodded to the lone room on the other side of the apartment. A bare, dark, glossy floor of wooden parquet squares shone in a room of white walls and a sliding glass door open to a narrow veranda. This was the room I would use for writing in the years to come.

"*Youshitsu desu*," he said, and with those words began my study of Japanese. That day, seeing my lack of comprehension, he was kind enough to translate.

"*Washitsu* means 'Japanese-style room,' one with *tatami* mats. *Youshitsu* means a 'Western-style room.'"

He smiled broadly.

"That is the Western room."

To work in Okinawa,
I rise before the light.
The window near the desk is black,
but dawn soon pinks the pane.

On the shadowed street below,
a taxi speeds by, roof light ghostly and green.

In the beginning,
gazing through glass at ordinary Okinawan streets
so strange in lines, design, orientation,
I can only wonder
how I will live in a nation
where the sun rises and sets in the sea,
furrowed blue foil
for an island, alone among a million people.

Even in my apartment, at my desk, early under glass,
I am the outsider
dark-eyed children departing in the dark of dawn
peer through bars to see.

Today, I will not write. I will walk
the narrow lanes of this once great kingdom
to *Shurijo*, high red castle on a distant hill.

•

I am dumb with longing to speak
to the ancient woman whose eyes I meet
as she creeps along, a bent black figure on a narrow winding way
bordered by six-foot gray cinderblock walls,
a street blinding with heat
where taxis slalom through telephone poles, dead cats, parked cars.

But I have no words,
and every driver sounds his horn
to wake me from my walk, to raise my eyes,
to signal my defeat, to wave them to a stop,
to sit in frigid conditioned air on corrugated-vinyl-sheeted rear seats
in red or blue or green or yellow or black cars for rent.

All wish for my admission that I'm lost,
in nameless, knotted lanes,
steep streets, and paved ways trailing away
like a sentence whose end is understood
and so unspoken.

None drive by
without an inquisitive hoot from the horn
to reveal a conviction
that I wander without direction in streets he calls home,
that I could never find my own way here,
could never find a place to call home here,
could never find my way home from here.

What is foreign stands alone.
Even within, outsiders remain outside.

I wind my way through strait, sunlit lanes,
and every driver knows
I'm lost.

●

Ezra Pound comes to Okinawa.
I'm his personal tour guide.

At Shurijo, once castle and capital of the Ryukyu Kingdom,
we stroll below the walls in the sacred grove.

Edging the waters of the royal pond
winds a broad path of carved coral limestone,
the bone of centuries of living creatures made stone
by generations building on death,
shining blocks cut from coral exposed in ebbing tides
and fit for walks and walls of white.

"When they dredged the pond of *Ryutan*,
gleaming waters emerald with algae,
the engineers sunk an eight-foot fence
of steel plates around the rim
in case of accidental detonation. Bombs fifty years old,
they said, lay moldering in shadowed depths."

Okinawa, Green Gem of the Blue World,
where every construction company
maintains a bomb-disposal unit.

"All the carp were killed, but not a single shell was found.
The stench of rotting fish filled the castle."

At our feet, green water clouds with reflected clouds
murky with light, flecked with golden motes
                    that may be dust, sand, or scales
            from pied, speckled carp scouring sunken stones
for bits of bread pinched from hot dog rolls by giggling children.

"Imported, I assure you, for the opening ceremonies
                    of this elegant, new museum,
            once a magnificent palace of maritime kings."

Pound stares at giant *koi* feeding in water so shallow
                            blunt backs break the surface,
scatter the sun's gold in a wet blaze of orange, white, and red
            in a silent green pond reflecting clouds and sky.

On Okinawa, there are more shades of blue in the world
                    than days anyone can count on.

                        ●

                                        taking Ezra by the ear

"In fact, the tale is often told to Okinawan children
                    of an ancient sleepy dragon
            who dwells in the depths of Ryutan
                in the dark where carp gleam gold.

Our myths cherish us,
and the dragon wards
all who believe.

"In rare moments, one glimpses
his private fire kindled within,
as the barred, wooden door of his submarine keep
swings wide
to let loyal and humble servants pass.

"The bombs no one ever found
are secure within his walls, gathered by the dragon
who treasures only grim metal shells of death,
a rusting hoard of perilous gems,
as another might guard gold,
watched not for their value but for ours."

●

What little I know of Japan will fill an unknown volume
of space with exponents, denominators, real and imaginary
numbers, constants:
a land ringing with bronze bells, honking taxis, firecrackers, hammers,
sonic booms, cicadas, and a sense of place
arising from no earth any man stands on.

Where does anyone stand
who stands here?

Am I lost or simply unfound on this strip of sand?
Hey, look, Japan! I'm an Oriental Accidental,
                    blown in from the northeast by storm,
    and the screaming steel bird who landed me here
                        was clearly a cuckoo
                        or a cowbird.

                            •

    "If you look directly ahead, Poet Pound,
                    you'll see before you *Shureimon*,
                entrance to the ancient capital city of Shuri.
    The name is often translated as 'Gate of Eternal Courtesy,'
            although I would rather say, 'Vigilant Decorum,'
                in the sense of severe and scrupulous observance
                    of formal and proper ceremony.

        "All who enter here
                are doomed
        to the rigid courtesies and stiff-necked respects
    of the Ryukyu Kingdom, and the Nation of *Nihon*
            which dominates from the northeast.

                            "Northeast, you may recall,
                is famed as the direction from which disaster advances,
                    and for the ancient maritime Kingdom of the Ryukyus,
                            this was all too true.

"Here, within a piked pale of politeness,
                    within the black lacquered walls
of the royal red hall newly-restored fifty years
                    after the typhoon of bombs and steel,
a distinguished visitor must uncomfortably sit, knees knotted
on finely-woven *tatami* mats in the Place of Honor,
                    confined by the refined
culture of two thousand years."

Pound ignores me,
        flipping pages in a dictionary of Chinese characters,
                    seeking the ideogram sporting his initials.

He'll place it prominently on his own turtleback tomb
                    as a sign, a stamp, a seal on his bones,
that outstrips the ragged verse at Shakespeare's grave.

            Orient visitors will nod and whisper,
            "*Inshouteki na hito desu ne.*"

●

English 1
Kyouyobu 3-303, Ryukyu Daigaku, Nishihara, Okinawa

From the window, I watch Ryukyu swallows
                whip through rain, wind, and walls,
arcing without bending wings,
                    over and around,
blue backs bolt between buildings.

My students recite English at my back,

        working hard to grasp my language

             by the roots.

      The tongue takes a long time

          to work out the words

        stuck in the head.

●

                Iso-Hiyodori *(Blue RockThrush)*

      I come to live on the island of Okinawa

          when I am half the age I will ever be,

turning thirty-five on this planet

        in the steaming heat of summer,

      season of paradox, surging and centering.

Now, on the rocky cliff of the coast,

        beneath white claws curling on waves,

          I see deep blue in deep waters,

        the long blue dye of Ryukyu indigo

    in cloth cut on this island a hundred years ago.

   In the turbulence of the pacific, I find *iso-hiyodori*,

        hermit of the surge

        centered

      on the edge of the sea.

Iso-hiyodori speaks what I never thought I would hear
everywhere,
strong song
in hedges of hibiscus behind crowded, towering buildings,
in straight slender branches of Ryukyu pine,
on slow curving walls of Zakimi Castle,
on the concrete ledges of windows where I work
overlooking my long view of the Pacific.

At Bolo Point, I see *iso-hiyodori* big as a robin,
blue, perched on the highest solitary rock
over the East China Sea
two hundred feet straight down and singing
knowing waves breaking
caves in the cliff below and spraying white plumes fifty feet
back over waves arriving
are nothing more than natural.

Here is a myth I make today.

Born on the crest of the curling wave
poised and free on the weird, bubble-pocked, vertical shocks
of sunned and water-worn coral,
trimmed in the actual blue of the sea
and earthy red shades of strange wave-cut shapes,
iso-hiyodori rings this place with song
among surging elements of salt, wind, rock, and sky.

●

Mr. Pound on the castle grounds

"*Kankaimon* is the main gate of Shuri Castle.
The name translates as simply as 'Gate of Welcome'
or as poetically as 'The Arch of Joy at Greeting.'
Here, outer walls open to the world,
so the entrance is flanked by *shisa*,
stone guardian dogs with blank eyes and ferocious faces."

Shisa bear witness to the essential
complementary in the East, which their postures prove.
One barks, one balks, one fierce, one fears. One thoughtful,
one thoughtless, one speaks, one silences speech.
Each calls for the other, and we must pass between.

"Overhead, stone arches
the entrance, as a silent weight of years spans the moment,
and please note,
Kankaimon faces west, to China,
first of three nations to demand tribute of the Ryukyu Kingdom."

Pound muses aloud,
"We face the gate that faces west."

"True, and we walk east to enter."

•

Tongueless on Okinawa, I address myself to America:

My fellow citizens,

Living far from America is strange. In some ways, I feel now I've never seen the country of my birth. America is a mythical place, a land of legend, and to some people here, I glow with an other-worldly nimbus, yet I didn't earn this supernatural awe, since for me as well, America is now a dream, a memory, distant in time and space, unknown but through images, and the images of America here are far from the ones I recall. A lens of space and time distorts distant lands and charges the sea between this nation and the other with monsters and magic isles. Distance mystifies and mythifies.

In the terminology of the cartographers, the entire island of America is "P.D.": "position doubtful."

Worse, every day I face my own illiteracy, frightening and fascinating. I know I can read, yet everywhere I look is indecipherable script. My own language I hear and see at random, garbled, isolated among exotic characters, strange even from those who learned my language in that far, fair country.

Here, I'm more helpless than a child, since a child breathes the language he hears, barred from reading only by a long labor of recognizing characters with sounds familiar to the ear. Yet I can question neither the signs nor the writing on the walls since I am not simply illiterate in this land, I am mute.

Laughing
children tangle me in long
spoken ropes of sound,
knot me with syllables,
surround me, pointing, giggling, tilting
dark heads together, whispering
what all can see
"Gaijin, gaijin."

Strange speech flows past my ears
hearing only the sea in shells
and surf sounding the shore of an island unknown
to one who simply wakes there walking
an untrod beach fresh after storm,
the wrack, the wreck, and the arrival
of a lost traveler from an antic land
deaf and dumb, afoot on the sand.

In this land, I am the outsider
the illiterate, the mute,
the village idiot grinning foolishly in the town square,
red-ribbed with the incomprehensible,
bound in tangled strands of foreign sentence,
in a world turning away
from me
dumb as a post
decorated, designed, described
by all around me,
all beyond me.

Here I am
the foreigner.

•

From Japan, America is the land
of the rising sun, inscrutable
with motives for war, never at peace
with the land or the world, always
lost in the flickering glare
of movies — the lights, the cameras, the action —
a vision
of fifty stars of plenty, paved with interstate highways,
banked and broad, naturally designed
for national defense.

In Japan, we drive roads
knotted through green or stript red hills,
jammed with colorless cars.

A compact car nation of incomprehensible traffic
in courtesy and a confusion of rules and signs
everybody knows a little,
and nobody knows completely,
and somebody long dead legislated before the automobile was invented.

"Japanese are obsessed with order, but they have no logic,"
says the Canadian.

Drivers park in the street, on the sidewalk,
on crosswalks, in the mouths of alleys,
driveways, entrances and exits, on the corner of the *koban*,
and idle for hours, asleep in the cool of a car,
near weedy, gray tombs
in canefields where bombs lie live beneath red soil.

•

The character of Japan is clear,

at least,

in the beverage of choice, *ocha*, tea, bitter and green,

with the brackish savor of tinted water

in an old pond

seasoned by the swift, silent passage of an elusive frog.

•

"That is *Zuisenmon*,

third gate on our tour,

second castle gate, and first gate within the walls.

"This is the 'Gate of Lucky Waters,'

for here, to our right, is *Ryuhi*,

a spring of turquoise-tinted water

flowing from a spout fashioned as a dragon's head

and overflowing a deep, square-walled cistern

reserved exclusively for the Ryukyu monarch."

All the somber-suited guards are elsewhere.

I fill the bowl of my hands at the dragon's lip

and sip the sky-colored water of kings.

Ezra glances nervously around.

He's not thirsty.

•

The Australian sums up the study of Japanese:

"If you speak the language,
      Nihonjin don't understand you.
If you don't speak the language,
      Nihonjin don't understand you.
If you err with the language,
      Nihonjin laugh, cover their smiles,
elbow each other, and point at you together."

Still, English, as we never knew it, is popular here
      although the syntax is foreign,
and the T-shirts incomprehensible: "literally and in all senses."

Weirdly-worded, 100% cotton communications
madden persnickety English teachers into sputtering
      fits of grammar, punctuation, and diction.
In this language, usage is use, and English only a design motif.

Amused by irregular sounds and shapes, syntax wanders,
denotation detonates, and chance words become poetry
      in fractured sentences
neither *nihonjin* nor *gaijin* read nor recognize.

In Japan, it simply takes a long time to learn English
is a very foreign language.

＊

In a Japanese tale I once heard,
a blind boy followed dark, beautiful music to a tombyard
and sat through the night embraced by ghostly airs.

Morning sun and weeping parents found the boy dead
seated on stone, smiling at songs
no living soul will ever hear.

The moral: stay far from words and music.
They enchant. They steal your life away.
They leave you cold and dumb as stone.

Listen late only to songs distant in the dark.
Heed the music where song is sweet,
but words are lost on the wind.

＊

"Before us is *Roukokumon*,
the 'Gate of Flowing Hours,'
or if you will, 'Gate of Dripping Minutes,'
for here, the flight of time was once marked
with a water clock,
measured drops on a human loom of liquid.

"This tiny courtyard encloses a secret of human dimensions,
for to heighten the castle's majesty,
there is some architectural sleight of stone.

"Within the walls, gates and turns are many,
        as one approaches the kingdom's heart,
    so the journey grows long through a little castle.

"Each gate is higher than the last.
      Long stairs slant down, steepened to lengthen steps,
        and a scant climb seems greater.

    "Enclosed courtyards are broad at entry
but narrow near the next gate,
        so portals loom larger, higher, grander,
   and enclosure makes walls taller
    by allowing only a view of the sky's Ryukyu blue.

    "Such are the stratagems that magnify the minute."

      ●

scenes of life in the quondam capital

    From the Western room, it's clear
        I live in the East.

   Through the year, I watch the scarlet blaze
      of hibiscus within dark
        green leaves.

  The first fortnight of every January, sudden pink petals
      of cherry blossoms
   blow from branches scraping cinderblock walls
    under steely skies of winter rain.

"petals on a wet black bough" —
accurate, if not exact
to specifications

Cherry blossoms white
in the Eight Islands of Japan,
but all those similes of snow,
the wayward drift and fleet passage of life,
ring false in southern isles.

Here on Okinawa, among the other lesser unnumbered isles,
frail blossoms mysteriously redden.

Taxis hiss through narrow, glossy lanes black as lacquerware
as petals leak pink in dripping rain.

Oh, Japan! Black suits, gleaming umbrellas,
and pink cellular phones in crosswalks!
A tedium of technology defeats the season.

●

I'm not only *gaijin*, "foreigner," and accidental expatriate,
but snagging the corner of the International Date Line,
I've turned inside-out, inverted, lost a day I won't see for years:

I'm the "inside-outsider,"
one with internals reversed, heart
on my chest, tongue uprooted, skin hidden within,
a dimensional man, peeled like an onion,
lung, muscles, blood, guts obvious and obscene.

Unseen, in Japan,
I live "outside" the world my neighbors know,
float the street we share tucked in a tough bubble of Westernity,
an elastic skin of separation as iridescent and varied
as a soapy globe.

I'm on the inside looking out
at the outside of Japan concealing orient pearls I will never see.
Behind the *noren*, behind pebbled glass and drawn curtains
and the sudden thunder of rolling glass doors with electric eyes,
is the Japan every *gaijin* believes
but never sees.

I'm the inside-outsider
left out in the rain on the curb of a ritzy *sushi* bar
refusing me entrance "solely on the basis of national origin,"
my taxi already sunk in the gaudy stream of night traffic
and dark waves of heat and exhaust
on International Street.

Hey, I'm an *American*!
You know, freedom and democracy
with liberty and good will to men?

I'm the inside-outsider,
peering through a foggy porthole in a damp, wooden door,
at Japanese faces dining in dimness within,
whose mouths open and close
as they savor the nameless in my absence.

I am the inside-outsider
collecting a scatter of black pearls before a locked door
in the artificial light of day.

•

Koufukumon, "Gate of Gracious Fortune,"
faces a wide, blue, spacious view over the city of Naha,
      a grand expanse of the East China Sea.

The gate also houses the ticket window:
      a thousand yen a head
for admission to the new museum of ancient empire.

I pay for two. Ezra, disoriented
      by heat and sky and sun,
snatches my change and peruses the cash for clues.

"The Japanese study the reverse
  of the *gozen-satsu* and see themselves
    a civilization on the edge
of a vast central emptiness of waves
  so powerful they keep a constant vigil on the ocean.

"In Japan, the sea is feared. Hokusai clawed
and fanged the swells towering over
  slender Japanese hulls obscured by the water's height.
    Every wave was Mt. Fuji enraged.

"Sixty-six percent of once wild coast is now fortified with seawalls,
  surf smashed and crashing,
    tides broken with concrete 'jacks'
      bigger than Toyotas
in a grim game of controlling elements."

Ezra stares at the broad, brown Pacific on the back of the bill.

"And, remember, that's *my* 5,000 yen, Buster."

●

Is this simply a nation of wrapping the insignificant
          in the extravagant, seamless pleats and creases
of culture fashioned from the rough, gaudy cloth of time?
    A nation where courtesy is a matter of form
          and formality is a mask
veiling the inappropriate gift, the unpardonable gesture,
        the bent history
    revealed in every figure, face, and fold?

      On the streets nobody knows
what to do next — except to shove the one in the way
    when the light changes
        and the call of the sidewalk cuckoo wakes the blind
to a chance to crowd through broken traffic in the street.

      At the bus stop on International Street,
          I pause at the open door
      as a few passengers step down,
and behind me, a wizened old lady —

                Little, yes! Tiny!
        Old? Oh, ancient, wrinkled persimmon of woman!

      — presses each palm to my pants
and pushes hard enough
    to move me.

●

Twilight opens the sky
to a universe of stars as a dark eye
opens to truth.

One evening,
in the moment when the moon rises full
and the solitary western sun bleeds away,
I glimpse the strange and fleeting poise
I must maintain here
among grave motions and great masses.

A scarlet wheel of sun balances
a silver ring of moon
over darkening deeps
of the blank, unfathomable blue
of sky and sea.

I spy the sun through a lens of moon.

●

"What I remember of Okinawa is clouds."
— Gary Snyder

Okinawa is a kingdom of clouds.
Swift, molten, blazing through blue,
there is no permanence in the white wisps winding through sky.

This green isle, this weedy bit of floating rope
between bowls of blue, sea and sky lip to lip,
is yet another cloud adrift.

We ride a wave-tossed raft of rock within reflecting heavens
Okinawans call "the blue world."

●

Ezra and the egg in Asia

"I contemplate and sting myself,
born blank in the Western world where white
means colorless, transparent.

"Not *tabula rasa*. Void,
devoid of distinction, distinguishing marks, expressionless.
Empty, featureless, bald as the sea, smooth,
ovoid as any egg
and equally, nakedly white."

Ezra and I stand at *Houshinmon*,
'Gate of Reverence and Service to the Gods'
who, in these isles, include the Three Fundamental Elements,
the First People, all ancestors, and one's own parents.

This is the greatest of the seven gates of Shuri Castle
through which we will pass.

"I am an egg in Asia,

pointless, boundless, rocking in wobbly circles,

reeling on an unpredictable, elliptical path.

"My heritage, if there is one,

is lost in a dark land beyond the Pacific

after winging my way west to the East,

a legacy shucked and chucked unlaced in rubbish piles of the past

like scuffed, crack-leather shoes

worn through the sole to the flesh

by thoughtless generations

who tore their tongues out long ago,

discarded with shards of starred eggshell,

orange rinds, coffee grounds, potato peels

tossed on the stained and aged, threadbare, unfashionable cloak

I will want later,

but too hot now to wear another moment.

Do I pale with 'ethnicity envy'?

"The rattling tongues of my neighbors

tease my ear, and I can guess what they're saying,

'Oh, those *gaijin*. They all look alike.'

"What a world to be white in!

If ever I crack this shell,

I'll flex pale feathers, pluck a quill from my wing,

and write till the red runs out."

A cracked American egg wobbles the walks of the castle keep,

and Ezra rambles to the grass and sits.

He's hungry.

We eat *tamago gohan* for lunch on the sunny green
by the grand wooden gate:
fried egg mixed with rice,
a dash of *shoyu*:
a simple dish of joy at noon.

"Ha! If I'm an egg,
there's life in me yet! My shell may be thin and brittle,
but I'm hard-boiled with a cheesy gold heart.
I'm edible and delicious. I'll make myself
palatable, comestible, digestible."

●

A Recipe for Scrambled American

one *arumi furai pan*
sesame oil
cooked rice
cold leftover vegetables
shoyu
salt
pepper
one American egg

Measure two tablespoons of sesame oil into the pan. Turn the heat high. When the oil smokes, spoon in cooked rice, and when that's hot, add the vegetables. Stir thoroughly until everything's steaming.

Crack the egg on the edge of the pan, plop the glop on top, poke the yoke, and stir the stuff till yellow flecks of dry, cooked egg appear within the roughage and white.

Sprinkle soy sauce till the rice tans. Salt and pepper to taste.

Serves over six billion.

●

ten, chi, umi

In Okinawa, these are the three ancient elements:
sky, earth, sea.

The Chinese and the Japanese
teach the basic elements are
sky, earth, and *man*.

On this green island
suspended in a blue world,
we learn the human
is not an essential element of creation.

One could live long at peace in such a place.

ten, chi, umi

●

Beyond *Houshinmon*,
Ezra and I wander the broad bands of brick
ranged in red and white rows of celebration,
in the *Una*, the great central courtyard
before the *Seiden*, the main royal hall.

"The Culture Committee rebuilt the walls, renovated the grounds,
and restored the shattered castle of five centuries of kings,
and here, at last,
is the gleaming, red, three-tiered, wooden heart
of the Ryukyu Kingdom."

"Make it new,"
says my occidental tourist.

"Razed twice by fire and once by bombs,
these brilliant scarlet walls are once again raised
beneath new clay tile the burning red hue of Ryukyu soil
and the sacred white of marine limestone mortar
with nine guardian dragons of wood and paint and stone and gold."

The poet pauses on the *Una*,
where ceremonies of kings were celebrated through centuries,
and the bronze bell of peace
cast five hundred years ago in a kingdom
known as the "Bridge of Nations"
was once buried in the rubble of war.

"It's hot," says Ezra.
His sweat spots red brick black in the sun.

●

M reports a taxi driver asked if she had a Japanese boyfriend.

When she said no,
he laughed and held his little finger erect.

Ah, sou desu ka?

In Japan, one more nation dominated by myths of size,
　　　　twisted trees are meticulously tortured,
miniatures of all sizes flourish, diminutive intricacies,
　　　　　　exquisitely minimal portions of odd foods,
　　cramped rooms, low doorways,
　　　　　　　dwellings and streets scaled small
　enough to knot a Western head,
　　　　and, then, that giant GNP, global corporations
　spanning lands on which the rising sun never sets.

　　All is tiny or towers in Japan,
　　　　little built to human scale.

●

　We saunter through the last gate,
　　a stone arch in a tilting castle wall,
　　　Kyukeimon,
　which I choose to translate as "Gate of Perpetual Gladness."

　　　"A quirk, I know, but it's an attitude
　　　　　toward life I've acquired living here,
　a willingness to encounter, to engage, to endure,
　　　　in a world that refuses to either notice or ignore me,
　　insisting on perspectives over my head,
　　　　behind my back, and out of my hands."

　　Ezra's bored. I'm babbling.

"Understand me. I'm glad
I no longer believe my presence will change everything.
On this side of the world, I've become one
who wishes for more:
that my presence might change little,
that I might dwell within what is
as what is, is."

Ezra glances back at castle walls,
all graceful waves and gentle slopes, a fortress
built by an architect with an artist's heart,
and stumbles on slanted stairs.

●

elegy in a distant country tombyard

Grass grows wild and high, but from the shore I see enough to know
what in the world this place contains.

Is there a lonelier sound than breezes through palms and Ryukyu pines?
On a cool blue tropical day, the wind is white noise
through leaves and needles, sand and strand.

The roof of the tomb arcs like a shell, a shape I'm told
recalls the long life of the turtle
in the design for the last humble house of ancestors,
walls of white coral in a land where white is the color of mourning.

None envy the dead, so we raise tombs to keep the peace,
where we gather Spring days, cut the weeds of years away, and picnic
through afternoons gone too soon.

Still, from where I sit in sunlight, the walls and curve
of the tomb's arching roof writes *omega*
on the weedy beach. *Omega*, end of a journey from womb to tomb.

Does the shape ensure life after death is eternal? Or is death alone
eternal? Is this good news? The character is a paradox
built of coral limestone blocks:
the end is eternal.

Every cut stone hewn for the tomb, every grain, shell, and stone underfoot,
even this hill beneath a sky that will never be blue forever,
will disappear in tides more profound than those on the shore.

Mountains and monuments are not eternal. Not even the sea will last,
yet the eternal remains, a swift cloud in the thought of an animal
too strong to bear the weight of the word
and too weak to smile at shifting glimpses of the rush through blue.

●

On the first night of the New Year,
we all hope to dream one of three lucky dreams.

The luckiest dream of Mt. Fuji,
in whose misty heights all wishes come true.

The less lucky dream of eagles,
for soaring wings bear wishes to the gods.

The last of the lucky
dream of eggplants.

Why?   No one can say.

●

On a bus in Kyoto,
a high-school baseball team of forty players,
forty other dreary evening riders, and two gaijin.

The boys are wild with the game,
silver, blue, and white, trim in uniforms.

Standing in the aisle, they wave gloves, masks, hats,
and swing bats till one whacks an old man in the ear.

Blood blooms like a scarlet flower,
soaks his collar, awes onlookers to silence
till one of the team giggles.
Then, the bus chokes with laughter.

I sneak the old man a handkerchief,
but seeing my face, he refuses.

That day, I saw *Kinkakuji*,
but all I recall of Kyoto is a long bus ride through dusk.

•

After the blank, blazing coral steps of *Kyukeimon*,
we pass a parking lot steaming with huddled buses and taxis idling,
sun sparking from every shining curve,
as I lead Ezra to my favorite spot.

"Of the seven gates of Shuri Castle,
here is an eighth, entrance to *Enkakuji*, a royal temple
in miniature, homage to Kamakura.

"I only tour the castle
with visitors from America and other foreign lands,
but I often come here,
for this place is a palace of paradoxes I've learned to savor.

"Look. The temple grounds are without the castle
but within the castle grounds,
beyond a gate without walls,
always locked, one through which we will not pass but pass around.

"See what I mean? Enigma flourishes here.
Only a decorative, black, wrought-iron fence a child could climb
guards sacred grounds eclipsed with weeds.

"The lotus pond was dug in 1498,
and the bridge crosses the mirrored water of further wonder,
for the bridge spans a pond
built solely for a bridge to span.

"Past the bridge are ancient stairs that rise to a parking lot
where pillars and roof once rose to blue,
for the bridge and pond survived the bombs, and the gate was rebuilt,
but the temple never was.
Where the sacred stood, now rests the technological, hot and idle.

"But what is gone when only a replica of what survives is lost?

"So, sir, we'll turn away from this emptiness
and gaze back.
There is a bridge of five centuries for a temple fifty years gone.

"Bridge and pond are all that survive
a temple destroyed decades ago,
leaving only a riddle
in a knot of bridge and pond to ponder."

Ezra muses in silence.
Maybe he contemplates a vow like mine:

Through that dragon-wrought knot, I will pass,
tracing every loop, curl, and weave on the way,
for a knot is yet a single strand, one line,
impenetrable, impassable only to those who will not pursue a path
through every twist, coil, and turn
to where it leads.

●

On Boy's Day, red, blue, and black streamers
in the mirror-spangled shapes of carp, open-mouthed
                    and astonished with ceremony,
    are raised on every house with a son under the roof,
            and I learn still more.

        The Japanese tell a Chinese tale
                to encourage their boys:
    the shy, little carp who climbs a waterfall to the sky
            becomes a gleaming dragon of fire and cloud.

            No fish of the Ryukyus,
    even in royal Ryutan, will ever strive at such a task,
    for no cascades tumble from these tiny heights, and the waters
            rise from a secret spring below.

Across the street, a happy, old Okinawan man sells ice cream cones,
                shaking hands solemnly
            with every American who dares
            order food with a foreign tongue.

He scoffs at the legend of the carp. One seeks such strength in vain,
        and the gaudy spectacle hides the truth
                    natives of this isle know well:
            strength abides in who survives.

•

Ezra demands to see fish, but will not wear a bathing suit.
　　　　　　　　　　　We accommodate him.

Pooling yen for a taxi, we four travel to *Busena-misaki.*
A hollow round steel shaft sunk in a living coral reef
　　　　　　　　　under forty feet of ocean
stands erect at the end of a narrow bridge over long water.

Within, we descend a double helix of spiral stairways
to portholes to peer through thick glass moons
　　　　　　　　　　into nearly natural ocean depths
　　as fish of many colors, many sizes, many forms
　　　　　　　　glide in silence beyond the glass.

We walk the circuit of clear, blank eyes three times,
sounding sparks of wonder with open vowels.
　　　　　　　Pound stares stonily at the floor of the sea.

As they gaze, the Japanese murmur the same word over and over.
　　It's familiar, but unfathomable, and I remark to M,
　　　　　　　　"Even the natives are impressed
　　　　　　with the beauty beneath the sea.
　　　Listen. They all say the same thing, '*Oishisou.*'"

M laughs loud, and others turn to stare.
　　　　　　"'*Oishisou*' doesn't mean 'beautiful.'"
She grins at rainbow shoals of fish adrift above flickering reef.
　　"What they're saying is 'Looks delicious.'"

Then, Ezra smiles.

●

Today, our taxi driver is Hitoshi.
He informs us seven times in flawless English syntax:
"I am Hitoshi."

"*Watashi wa Eriku desu. Hikoujyou ni ikitai.*"

"Oh, international terminal."

The words are katakanized:
intanashinaru taminaru.

"*Iie, kokunai no.*"
"No, the domestic one."

He smiles, aglow with mischief.
"Oh, you are going to *Japan.*"

"*Ima, doko ni desu ka?*"
"Where am I now?"

●

Awkward on the floor,
we are silent, seated on *tatami* with our counterpart couple,
glossy black *hashi* in hand, sharing raw fish, rice,
and sweat-beaded glasses of warm beer,
regarding each other face to face.

Across the apartment, the Western room is dark.

Over a low table of high polish, we wonder
what to say, wonder how to say something significant,
something beautiful to each other,
knowing, to the east, over the edge of the world is
America, rampant.

●

The carp is gold, but that's not enough.

In Japan, I learned,
the gilded fish who leaps from still green waters
to climb the fluted, white stairs of waterfalls,
will shed scales, sprout magnificent wings,
and mount the sky
for misty, rocky ramparts of clouds heaped in blue
like ruined walls of ancient castles.

Newborn, the dragon rises to vague, forgotten kingdoms
of dreams and shifting images
riding tides through the sky
and disappears forever and for all through high, broken castle gates
into vast, ambiguous realms
of white.

●

iii: THE RUSH THROUGH BLUE

Reckless as Botchan

Coming to Okinawa, I am reckless
as Botchan leaping from the second floor
proving he could fly without dying
or slicing a thumb to try the bite of the blade.

What do I know of Japan?
Nothing but my address in Shuri, the number of my bus,
how to apologize, count my change, excuse myself, greet my neighbors,
and who is on the thousand-yen bill.

The people who live here warn me, "You will never be Japanese."
Fine, but I know where I am.
I only want to be native anyway —
to drink *Orion* or *awamori* and watch the moon,
gaze into the green and deep dragon waters of *Ryutan,*
know the birds, the trees, the rivers, the back roads, and the beaches.

No matter how hard I scrub my feet in the public bath
there is American dirt worn into the heel.
I won't wear shoes here either.

I know I'll never walk down the street in my own neighborhood
without taxis tooting
or finding myself the point at the end of a child's finger —
a curious man from a curious land.

"That's the way it is," I say to the children
standing at the bus stop
staring at the sky in my eyes,
"you are what you are."

But when I go back to America, I want my face
on the five-dollar bill
just like Soseki on the *sen'en-satsu*.

Ear Shot

What pierces the ear opens the eyes.

A black and white bird with cumulus cotton-ball head
and a big voice wakes me:
"Koko ni, koko ni."

I wonder. "Where am I?"
Every morning, strange sounds around me.
A new world bangs by my window.

Clouds are low, scudding through blue in a vaporous rush.
Morning sun reddens
anonymous apartment blocks, cane fields, and a turtle-back tomb.
Okinawa at dawn.

Before public address systems boom
bombastic German symphonies,
before my busy ancient neighbor sweeps stairs at dawn,
before the early black Mercedes idles curb-side
for Mr. Big on the highest floor, this olive-backed bird
clamors in cane by my window.
Koko ni, koko ni.

Chinese Bulbul, are you here only to wake me?
Take care. Farmers will pop you with pellet guns.

Pow!
I'm shot through the head
with sound around here. Blood rushes to my ears
ringing with the rattle, crash, boom of morning in this place
I never thought I would ever be,
so foreign and so near.

In Japan, even the cock crows in another tongue,
and *shirogashira* speaks Japanese.

Koko ni, koko ni.
"Here," says the bird. "Here."

Within earshot, here is *all* I hear.
Koko ni, koko ni.

Alone In Our Own Latitude

in Japan with Veronica

Alone in our own latitude the way we are,
days are lazy, light blue on white sand, we are free,
living as we do because of the way we are.

Long purple-gold sunsets pierced by one evening star,
on a high hill with warm wine, we wonder to be
alone in our own latitude, the way we are.

Each day, foreign grows familiar; familiar, far.
Seeing us, our neighbors can't believe what they see,
living as we do. Because of the way we are,

we greet across a gulf where our words are a bar,
yet we know red hibiscus and blue sky agree,
alone, in our own latitude: the way we are.

Poised on wind, dragonflies. We sit late by the car
drinking wine near the knotty *gajumaru* tree
living as we do because of the way we are.

From this little green island, the west is too far
east to see past the blue curve of darkening sea —
alone in our own latitude the way we are,
living as we do because of the way we are.

On Listening to a Bootleg Recording
of Allen Ginsberg Reading *Howl* …

As I Eat a Blueberry Pop-Tart & Drink Instant Cappuccino
From a Mickey Mouse Mug
While Watching a Brilliant Yellow Bull-Dozer Clear Oil-Stained Earth
For Yet Another Grim Shoebox Apartment Building
And Glimpse Between the Corrugated Aluminum Supermarket Warehouses
& Vast Brown Weedless Field of a Car Sales Storage Lot
The Forlorn Gray-Green of Waves in the Haze
Beyond the Sea-Wall
Far from My Concrete Balcony
In Okinawa, the Last Prefecture of Japan

I never expected this to happen.

Hunting Hawks in Okinawa

Where hawks walk, wings will not wait for me to watch,
exploding from the branch with a cry, a curse.

Here, the hawk is food, and he flies.
Morning glories and mongoose be damned.
There is a man.

In the great golden valley of my country,
no one harries the hawk.

Still, these wings stay as I pass,
a cloud through a valley
sharper eyes see to the last blade of grass.

What would it take to make me
make a meal of hawk?

The hawk glares down
at the dust I raise walking,
gawking at the grim, shouldered shape on the limb.

That is my shadow there on the ground.
When it is gone, the hawk hunts.

After Ryokan: For a Distant Friend

I think of you, mountains
and rivers away, me beneath a crescent moon
     after three days darkness.

Night in summer, alone on a beach
    back against one of these tough trees
        nobody can name.
Black roots drive straight down through sand.

The ocean is black with white wings —
        water bending, breaking
    into surf, spray, drift, and dune.

The sand is cool, and there is time
        to watch the night
    turn through a slow dark circle
centered on a dim spark too far away.

The Milky Way reflects the path
      the moonlight makes on the sea.

I want to tell you something
I can't right now.

I can't write now.

I want to tell you something.

Paper

Here in a nation where neither of us read or write,
the gods are paper
inked in wild characters
their ministers interpret but do not understand.

In a culture of wrapping, paper is a cloak of strokes
that conceal as they reveal.
Every character is a portrait of the ineffable.
They are letters lost in transit.

Even our marriage certificate is a document
we cannot decipher, scripted in foreign characters
read from top to bottom, from right to left.

We hung the original in the only frame that fit the kitchen
and gaze over coffee at the fathomless glass face
every morning of the world.

The character of our union is lost
in bold black strokes on official blankness,
in red seals and stamps
ranked within a broad border of gold.

We see more than ink and paper, beyond words,
                    a sense unsuitable for framing,
reading more than one who only sees words
        written on paper will ever understand.

Asagi Triptych

I.   First and Final Asagi

The night of the final exam,
20th-Century American Literature class is silent
with the scratching of pens.
This is not a test.

II.   English as a Sound Barrier

Three languages at lunch on Okinawa,
yet no one at the table speaks. I break
the silence with words everybody knows.
No reply.

III.   Second Language Barrier

Syllables splash like rain. I'm lost in Tokyo.
Fingers point, umbrellas drip, hands wave,
words leak from my ears.
I understand Japanese perfectly.

In Lieu

Today, I seek a place secret to no one.

Encompassed by broad blue and the silver shadows of clouds on waves,
    I kneel in thick, damp, green growth on a sunny day
        in the rainy season, facing east beneath a huge banyan:
    one more spontaneous ceremony for one more gone.

Red roots dangle from limbs, brush my ear as I crouch
        over somebody else's cinderblock, a makeshift altar
    for burning *uchikabi* and incense from supermarket shelves.
    Uguisu warbles from shadows, song from a source unseen.

        Twenty-five years in a moment.
        A quarter of a century in one day.

Flames blacken brown paper and white smoke rises
        as I gaze far from the hills of Sueyoshi Park —
    through sky, wind, water, and time,
            you choose your own direction.

Among rocks, green, shadows, pine, and flashes of sun,
through mountain misery and manzanita,
                    your hands full of purpose,
        your head full of circles, and your heart simply full,

            you seek a place only you know now.

                Twenty-five years ago.
            I nearly forgot today was the day.

But this morning, cresting a hill where the sun rises from America
                over sugar cane, hog barns, and a bakery,
            there was a traffic jam on my way to work.

    Through lines of idling white cars, honking taxis,
                        and buses grinding gears,
        an old man, straw hat and faded red rag round his neck,
    led a blinkered chestnut mare pulling a splintered wooden cart
                up the slope of morning.

            He was backing up traffic in every direction
                    for miles.

Burning Earthward

Hot breeze, sun,
through long, wet hair cascading in brilliant rays
over the back of a chair.

Copper, gold, and silver tints
as wind warms what already blazes.

As you lean, the nature of hair gleams,
as neck tilts and strands fall free,
as fingers work water through,
as threads brighten and dry.

Your hair is a golden tear, a glowing tongue,
a flame burning earthward.

April Fool

A Minor Event on L-Day
April 1, 1945, Okinawa

with no apologies to history

A perfect day for an invasion, blue sky, calm sea, high tide,
      a swift force at dawn takes an undefended beach:
   men tense, shoulders hunched, stumble through surf
        into Japan, without firing a shot.

"April fool," whisper waves on empty beaches,
           "So far for so little."

   Two air fields occupied without opposition: the runways
        change hands without a gesture of defiance,
conquered so quickly not everyone gets the word.
      Okinawa glints green and familiar from the air.

"April fool," soldiers grin ruefully over smokes
           and rifles at rest.

At noon, a lone Japanese plane circles the field once
                    and descends to the narrow dirt strip:
                    a perfect landing in the last airfield he ever chose.
        Americans stare as the plane taxies to the nearest squad.

"April fool," whisper waves on empty beaches,
                            "So far for so little."

The pilot leaps from the cockpit and trots over. Only in his last step
        does the man see his mistake. A phrase of amazement
                escapes his lips, his eyes comic zeroes of wonder.
        Nobody speaks his language, and somebody shoots him.

Voice of Stone:
June 16, 1996, Peace Day on Okinawa

for #30571

The dead have forgotten us,
    but we cannot forget them.

This hot June day, we number rocks
to touch the dead fifty years gone —
    200,000 in a single season.
Some call that a battle.

  Sea, sand, grass, stone, sun.

We stack stones, pile them singly
    by the thousands,
hefting the dimensions of a loss
    grown vague in a waste of days.

Stone by stone, we discover the work
in writing on rock. The natural resistance
of the material dulls the point,
                    clots the ink with dust.

          The labor is not lost on us —
how much harder to die on such a day?

                Sea, sand, grass, stone, sun.

The elements are fierce here. Life
grows swiftly among glaring immensities,
                    and none wish for more than shade,
water, a little laughter.

The traffic blurs, close and quick,
                    but the blare of horns
is crushed beneath a high, heavy sky,
                    lost in heat and green.

What we hear is the first summer cicada
                    whirring in limbs overhead.

                Sea, sand, grass, stone, sun.

I picture one whose number I am
                    writing on rock: 30571.
With a single feature, a scent, one syllable
                    of a name now lost,

I want to say I remember
                one I never knew,
but in the sun I see today
                what is eternal is gone.

Sea, sand, grass, stone, sun.

On a still, searing day of peace,
                grief at the immutable drives us
                        to choose a pen
              to ink black figures on stone

for the unknown, across a broad green field
                bound by a deeper blue than sky.
On a horizon receding only from us,
the lost remain, changeless,

faceless, diminished in a distance of days,
              named now only with a number.

Wood

A living pine rocks on a coral limestone ledge, green
gone for the sky, blue
sea rumbles below, white whipped
from waves by wind,
and the breeze in the limbs
gives the tree voice:

a song that love lives long
in wind, ocean, rock, and pine,

a song of turbulent elements
the world makes one,
wed in root, trunk, limb, and leaf,

a song wind blows through
the blue world
in spindrift, bond of wind and wave.

We will last as long as wood lasts —
long enough, not forever,
as long as life lasts,
green on gray limbs over blue waves white on dark rocks.

Sajak Saja: Ubud, Bali

Gedé stops the car on a high hillside bridge
and points to the next panorama:
                a classic vista for visitors with cameras.

We step into the view, as he sketches in a notebook,
                                passing time as tourists tour.

He's been here before. The crowd of children
gathered on every bridge with a scenic view
        brandish the paintings and carvings of their elders,

who labor through night on works for tourists who buy nothing
                                and take only pictures.

Beyond painted scenes, in the valley below,
padi descend in trim terraces of green gleaming gold
                as sunlight glances from still surfaces.

A man in a red shirt works shin-deep in a muddy ricefield.
                Palms wave in a constant breeze.

The sky's blue is an elegant tropical afterthought
of gods who daily recreate creation. On this island everyone
masters an art, and even gods are artists.

The valley's green and gold graced the morning's dance,
and in the car, I speak a little poem aloud:

"Green *padi* gold in the sun —
shades from shining skirts
of *legong* dancers."

Gedé closes his book, content with what the windshield frames:
beyond small hands waving works of art

and faces pressed to glass, an original world
as green as an American dollar. He starts the engine
as I snap one last landscape shot.

What's one more pretty poem on an island of artists
in a world every dawn renews?

Orang Malu:
The Shock of Recognition

In Indonesia, wood carving is an art common to all,
and one of the most intriguing figures
is the orang malu, *the shy man.*

Devotion I: One And Many

Crude or polished, carvings crowd
            the marketplace
    near a fountain where a basin brims,
drops spill silver in the sun.

Hundreds of hunched little wooden men
    ranked in rows for foreign fingers
        seeking souvenirs.

Back curved, elbows furled, muscles taut,
        face hidden in hands
spread on knees, legs crossed beneath,

orang malu, the shy one,
is a knobby knot of man turned inward,
or away.

Raised to the light,
on an open palm,
the grain lightens and darkens
in the angle of the gaze.

Devotion II: One Among Many

On the sharp edges of leaves, drops of dew
too small to fall
disappear.

Held near the eye,
the *orang malu* is a plain figure,
one who sees
humanity means one *can* see oneself
as one
separate, alone.

Dew forms drops
that fall or fade.

Devotion III: One With One

"In Indonesian, shy *is a synonym for* wild*."*

Wild, *orang malu* never sees himself
    till one morning, near a waterfall,
he sees a stranger, and in the stranger,
        sees himself, alone.

He knots himself in a new world of one
    to restore one now lost within
a world at once grown greater and less.

    Enclosed, enfolded
as a surface of water, falling,
        tenses into a sphere,
    a shining drop in a sunlit cascade.

A man curled in a ball on the muddy bank:
    in the shy one, we see ourselves,
    the human shrinking from the human.

Devotion IV: One With Many

From a blue sky, rain.
The shy man sits, round as a raindrop.

In his image,
we mark the moment
one knows
one is
one of many.

Within the forest, among leaves, countless drops.
Orang malu, alone, drips with rain.

Devotion V: One Among Others

The *orang malu* is only human.
His feet are muddy. The waterfall
thunders in a green glade.

In the stranger he sees, he knows
he is not all there is. Hiding his face,
he faces nothing, cut from a world once one.

If humanity is a tragedy,
this is the moment of recognition,
and all is changed by revelation:

Knowledge knots the past, snares the future,
and rounds the present to a fluid sphere
falling silver through forest air.

All is clear and lost and passing
in dim shadows and green darkness.

The stream dances at his feet.
A thousand shards of day in a single rippled face.

Devotion VI. One Without Others

In a clearing flecked with sun, stands the shy man,
lone in a moment.

In a moment, the human becomes
human, for in this moment, first
in this moment, only,
does he see.

At his feet, a spring rises through roots and rock.
His moment is his alone.

Orang malu is the one without a name,
who for the first time,
knows he needs one,
and grieves the nameless now lost.

Devotion VII: One Within One

The fountain, a world in one,
overflows.

Lost, as we are when we seek to hide,
we seek a world of ourselves,
not seeking ourselves
in the world.

At our feet, by the fountain,
the earth,
where the water falls,
greens.

Hari Natal di Indonesia:
Kuta, Bali

On *Jalan Legian,* muddy street of schemes
    and baseball-capped vendors
                of cheap watches and perfume,
    the sky is sacred blue.

The sidewalk gleams with grime. Every dirty puddle
    shines. Every filthy inch of asphalt,
every fold in the tattered skirts of black and white
                wrapped at the waists
    of stone guardians at timeless shrines
glows in the boom of noon.

From the sidewalk, shops are dark,
                stark with shadow,
    but when we linger, voices call —

      "Hello."
           "Yes, have a look?"
    "Where are you going?"

Veronica unfolds *sarongs* of earthy tropical hues,
　　　　　rich, dark shades in sunlight,
　　　and jokes with a shopkeeper
　　　　　　in Indonesian.

"Ini suami saya," she says. I know the words,
　　　　　and I glance up.

He greets me, and appropriate to the day,
　　　I speak my little Indonesian,
　　　　　　"Selamat Hari Natal."

"Oh, *Meri Kerismas,"* he says,
　　　　　"and you are Christian?"

Surprised, I blink and look at the sky. This blue
　　　　　spans a land of ten million gods,
　　　yet every foreign face must follow only one.

Blue and yellow taxis honk in the streets.
　　　　　Motor scooters and buses blast by.
　　　I shake my head, searching for words
　　　　　　in his language or mine,
　　　but find none before he asks again.

　　　　"Buddha?"

I consider the endlessly amusing possibilities.
　　　　　Me, a Buddha?
　　　　But I must say no. *"Bukan."*

The shopkeeper frowns, confused,
                         but soon brightens.

          "Yes, Hindu."

O, land of boundless possibility! I swear
                    I will instantly convert!
      But I deny him again,
        "Maaf, Bapak, bukan."

Veronica explores racks and rows of clothes,
                  smiling at our slow words
         and finally speaks,
      "Bapak, dia tidak punya agamah."
        "Sir, he has no religion."

I'm astonished, amazed. No religion!
             Veronica laughs at my fallen face.

"At least tell the man I'm a poet," I whisper.
      She grins, "I don't remember the word."

Now, the shopkeeper smiles.
             He has an answer at last.
      "O, begitu," he says, *"Dia bebas."*
               "He's free."

Gekka Bijin:
Beautiful Lady in Moonlight

a ryuka for the Rock

After sunset, night-flowers bloom,
draw us into darkness, seeking
a source. Found by the fence, the scent
      fills our heads with the night.

Swimming in a Shirt of Sharks

Immersed in coral blue, sharks circle me
    on the weave of waves my collar crests,

        shark tails on shirt tails,
  pale gray images of liquid lightnings in the sea.

Salt stings my eye, but sweat tangs my tongue
    as triangular teeth seize a button or a cuff. I smile,

      beloved of deadly creatures,
        in whose dread images I dress.

In my shirt of the sea, I'm high and dry,
    striding through sky, surrounded,

    enclosed, encompassed, embraced
by sleepless predators of the deep.

Death Mask in Red
for Allen Ginsberg: April 5, 1997

Poetry is a stop sign —
>   either you get it or you don't.

Surprisingly few do.

After all, how many drivers
>   ever really come
to a complete stop?

A Portable Planet

from Shuri to Sarasota

Most of the time, we live on different days.
Our seasons match,
but your night is my day.

As I rise, you set a clock to wake you while I watch the sun set.
The only star you see when I sleep is the sun.
On New Year's Eve, we spend fourteen hours in different years.

For my birthday, you shipped an Inflatable Globe.
I unfolded seas and continents and wondered at a flat Earth.

A god who wanted everyone to see the same sun
would smash the planet to such a plane —
a single side, all edges, corners, and straight rivers.
Cartographers and generals would love it.

But the world I want is a ball,
tangled in the paradise of paradoxes
roundness generates.

So I blew it up and began to play.
The uses for a portable planet are endless.

With my fingers placed on our two towns,
I spin the globe on new poles,
a wacky axis for the plastic Earth to wobble on,
whirled without end.

Sometimes, I bounce the planet on my fist
with a rubber band looped through the North Pole.

And, yesterday, I arranged a rainbow
of plastic dinosaurs at the end of the hall
and bowled them over.

The world works really well this way,
with a little english on it.

Shakti

In her sleep, Veronica dances.
Her toes point, pivot,
and wake me.

That wild, glad urge
to suddenly spin in darkness

inspired the first step of Shiva's dance,
the one
that whirled the world in the beginning,
sparked stars aflame,
and brought tears to the green eyes of the universe.

On the Verge of the Usual Mistake

I learned the same thing on the beach again.
Between the sea and the land is a broad white span
                where the surf makes lines
                        and the lines are blank.
On the sand, hermit crabs, broken coral, and wave-worn shells,
        a cowrie with colors fresh from deeper water.

This is the margin change demands of the world.

In the surf, there is a distance before the coral grows,
        before the fish begin, where there is no rock or green.
The empty sand above and below the waves is the space
the tides mark for the moon. On the sea's blue edge
nothing grows, nothing rests,
                        nothing that comes here,
stays here.

Yadokari: Hermit Crab, Okinawa

He borrows his house, as I borrow mine.
         We are strangers where we live.

This little crab makes me think
I would crawl around the world with my belongings on my back,
    drag my life behind me every day,
        to live
in the same world of open sand, empty shells, brilliant blue.

In hand, the hermit crab lives up to the name,
       a shell closed with claws
    but a warm breeze of breath will bring him out.

Set on the shore, he works a way through humps of white sand,
broken branches of coral, sun-bleached beer cans,
       human footprints.

Life is kind. Move on. Carry what you can.

One Last Lesson from the Reef Egret:
The Instant of Recognition

Every day, at noon, when I cross the bridge on Okinawa
where the *Shirahigawa* meets the East China Sea,
ashen wings flap, and a sole gray bird
leaps into the air.
What the Reef Egret sees, it flees.

The flight of the bird saddens me,
and I admit the truth.

I once dreamed in Okinawa
the Reef Egret would someday see me
as familiar as low, rushing, tropical clouds,
as garbage and golf balls in shallow, gray water,
as dirty surf, as the muddy, rusted motor-scooter
half-sunk in the silt and stench of the river
where he perches
beneath the concrete and aluminum span of Japan.

No more.
This is one more place I do not belong.

Forget the silly, wishful dreams of scientists,
that we are not standing in our own way,
that we can watch without an effect,
that what we observe does not observe us,
that daily as I cross the bridge,
I am simply a slim glimmer of shadow in sun
on sand and sediment.

The clarity in the vision of the reef egret is rare,
and there is one last lesson for me here:
the lone gray bird feeding on this filthy river
recognizes what I am at once
and flies.

About the Author

Eric Paul Shaffer was born on June 3 on the Colonial Coast of America and traveled steadily westward until he reached the edge of the East, and lived for eight years on Okinawa, once the ancient island home of the Ryukyu Kingdom. Taking a new direction, he turned seaward once more and now lives on the most remote archipelago on the planet, two thousand miles of broad, blue waves from any continent.

He is the author of two previous books of poetry, *RattleSnake Rider* (1990) and *kindling: Poems from Two Poets* (1988, with James Taylor III), and a chapbook, *Instant Mythology* (1999). His work has been anthologized in *The Soul Unearthed* (Tarcher/Putnam), *Witnessing Earth* (Catamount Press), and *On Fry Bread & Poetry* (forthcoming from Longhand Press). His poetry has also appeared in *ACM (Another Chicago Magazine)*, *Asylum*, *Bakunin*, *California Quarterly*, *CQ: California State Poetry Quarterly*, *Chaminade Literary Review*, *Chicago Review*, *East & West Quarterly*, *Fish Drum*, *The MacGuffin*, *Pearl*, *Peregrine*, *Pleiades*, *Seattle Review*, *Snowy Egret*, *South Coast Poetry Journal*, *Stick*, and *Threepenny Review*, among others.

He also edited and wrote an introduction for *How I Read Gertrude Stein*, a study of the works of Stein by Lew Welch, which was published by Grey Fox Press in 1996. He is currently at work on *Lew Welch*, a study of the life and works of Welch, for the Western Writers Series of Boise State University.

Living at the Monastery, Working in the Kitchen, his next book of poetry, contains poems written in the persona of Shih-te, seventh-century Chinese cook and janitor at the Buddhist-Taoist monastery of Kuo-ch'ing in the T'ien-t'ai Mountains in China during the T'ang Dynasty. Friend to the famed Han-shan (Cold Mountain), Shih-te wrote barely half a hundred poems, and these works give further voice to his life and experience. *Living at the Monastery, Working in the Kitchen* will be published by Leaping Dog Press in the Spring of 2001.